The Same But Dif

by Jillian Powell

Contents

Longman

Edinburgh Gate
Harlow, Essex

Sarah Is Deaf

Sarah likes dancing and she is learning to ride a horse.

When Sarah was six, she had mumps. She got better but the illness made her **deaf**. Sarah's mum and dad knew something was wrong. They took her to have hearing tests. The doctors found out that Sarah's illness had left her deaf.

At first it was hard for Sarah. She could not talk easily to her mum and dad, or her friends. She found it extra hard when she was in a noisy room, such as a classroom with lots of other children.

Now Sarah goes to a school for the deaf. She wears a tiny hearing aid. This makes sounds louder so she can hear more easily.

Sarah has learned to **lip read**, too. Sarah watches people's lips to make out the words they are saying. It helps when people speak clearly because this makes it easier to lip read.

Sarah has also learned to **finger spell**. She has learned the finger-spelling alphabet. She can use her fingers and hands to spell out words.

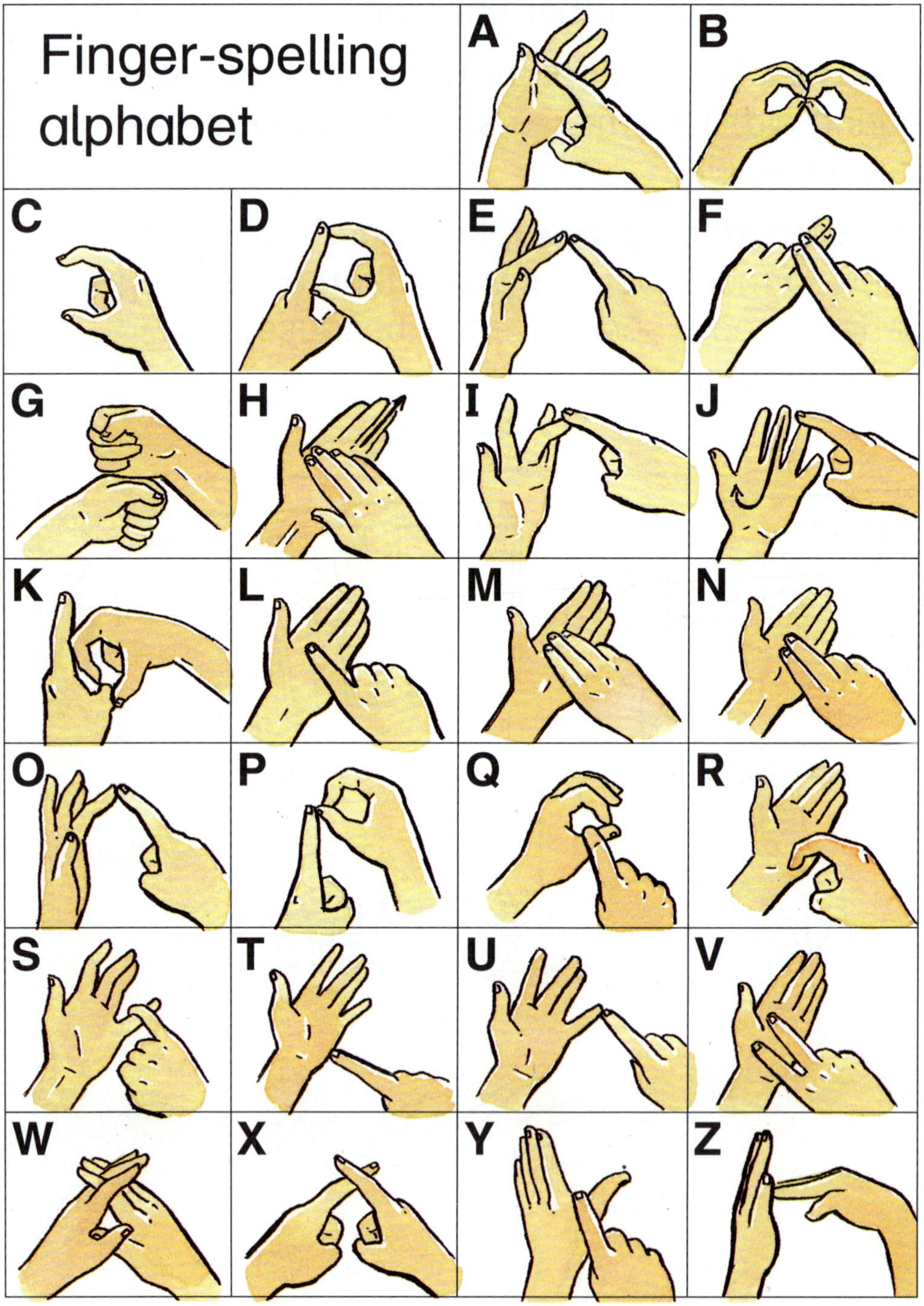

It is hard for Sarah to use a telephone so at home she uses a **text phone**. She types out the words she wants to say on the telephone. She can chat to her grandparents on the text phone.

Sarah watches television with the rest of her family. Sometimes, the TV programmes have **subtitles** so Sarah can read words as they are spoken.

Sarah wants to work with horses when she is older. She would love to have her own pony one day.

Andrew Has Spina Bifida

Andrew likes playing basketball, and playing games on his computer. Sometimes he swaps computer games with his friends. Then they can all try new games.

Andrew has **spina bifida**. This means that when he was a baby growing inside his mother, his **backbone** didn't join up properly. Spina bifida is sometimes called 'open spine'.

People who are born with spina bifida can't use all their **muscles** properly. Andrew's spina bifida means he can't walk easily. When he was a baby, Andrew had to have operations on his back and his feet. It meant he spent quite a lot of time in hospital. Andrew can't wriggle his toes or bend his ankles.

The doctors gave him special **braces** to wear on his feet to help him stand and walk.

Now Andrew has learned to walk with sticks to help him. When he wants to go faster, he uses a **wheelchair**. He plays wheelchair basketball and other sports. Andrew also loves riding his bike. His uncle changed the pedals on his bike so he can ride it safely.

Andrew goes to the same school as his sister, but he goes in a taxi instead of catching the school bus.

He goes to the same classes as the other children, but when they are doing games he uses the machines in the gym instead. These help him make his muscles stronger.

When he is older, Andrew wants to invent computer games.

Joshua Is Visually Impaired

Joshua loves music. He is learning to play the piano and the violin, and he sings in two choirs. His favourite composer is Scott Joplin.

Joshua is eight years old. When he was six weeks old, doctors found out there were problems with his eyes. Some people are born with this disability. It is called **visual impairment** and it means Joshua cannot see properly. He can see colours but he cannot see shapes clearly. Joshua uses colour to help him. He looks carefully at people's clothes so he will remember what they are wearing. This helps him to recognise people.

At school, Joshua has special helpers. His classroom helper copies things down for him from the blackboard in big letters which he can see. Joshua also has a helper who takes him out and helps him learn how to get around safely.

When Joshua is out shopping with his mum, he wears a badge to tell people that he is visually impaired. This is because Joshua often likes to pick things up and touch them, because he can't see them clearly.

At home,
read all
Harry Pot

Joshua is learning to type. He uses a computer with a specially clear screen. Joshua can also use a talking calculator to help him in maths classes. He already has a talking watch which tells him the time.

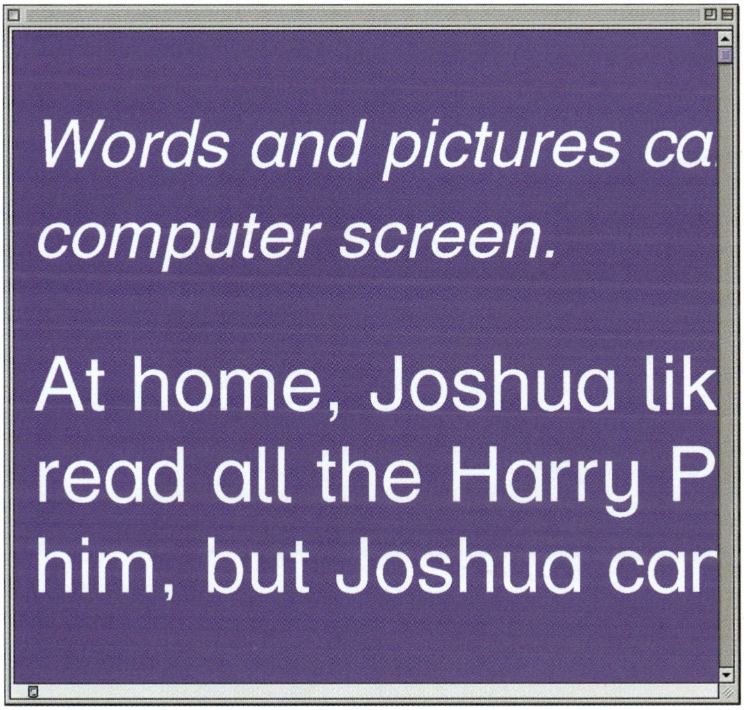

Words and pictures can be magnified on a computer screen.

A talking watch

At home, Joshua likes reading. His mum read all the Harry Potter books aloud to him, but Joshua can also read them himself in big print. He also likes paintings. He gets special pictures out of the library called "**thermoforms**" that he can feel with his hands. They come with tapes that he can listen to while he is feeling them.

Joshua has always wanted a dog. He and his mum sponsored a dog at the Dogs' Rescue Centre. They used to go to visit him and take him for walks. Now they have given a new home to a dog from the centre. Joshua has called him Lento, which is a word from music which means "slow"!

Joshua likes going to the theatre to see musicals with his mum. They sit in the front row so Joshua can see the stage clearly. He can see best when they sit on the right hand side of the stage and look to the left.

When he is grown up, Joshua wants to be a musician. He thinks he may play the piano or be a composer.

Alex Has Cystic Fibrosis

Alex is seven. She likes reading and painting pictures. She likes choosing her own books to read from the school library. She also has lots of teddy bears. Her teddy bears are all different sizes and colours.

Alex has **cystic fibrosis**. She calls it "sixty-five roses" because that is what it sounds like when mum says the words. Some people are born with cystic fibrosis. Alex's parents found out she had it when she was a baby. When Alex was a few months old she had problems **breathing**. At first Alex's mum and dad thought she had a cold. Then the doctors did tests and found out that cystic fibrosis was making Alex **wheezy**.

At first, Alex's parents did not know what having cystic fibrosis meant. The doctors explained that when someone has cystic fibrosis, salt and water are not carried round their body properly. Their skin can get very salty and their **lungs** can fill up with a sticky stuff that makes it hard for them to breathe.

Sometimes Alex coughs a lot and feels wheezy. Cystic fibrosis also makes it hard for her body to **digest** food properly. Alex often feels hungry but she doesn't put on much weight. She has to take special medicine to help her body digest her food.

Alex has to have treatment every day to stop her lungs filling up with sticky stuff. This is called her "chest PT" or **chest physical treatment**. Alex lies down on her bed or on the sofa. Then her mum taps all over her chest and back to clear the sticky stuff out of Alex's lungs. Alex is used to PT now. She doesn't mind because it makes her feel better. She always puts her favourite music on so she can listen while she is having her PT.

Vitamins A and D

Vitamin E

Cystic fibrosis makes it hard for Alex to fight off **germs** and **infections**. Her mum makes sure that Alex has lots of vitamins to keep her healthy. But when Alex does get sick, she has to take special drugs to help her body fight back. Sometimes, she has to go to hospital. She always takes her favourite teddy bear with her. The doctors give her medicine to make her better.

Alex wants to work in a library when she is older. She wants to be able to choose all the books in the library!

PUGWASH

Danny Has Diabetes

Danny is eight years old. He is a football fan and he supports his local team. He goes to all their matches with his dad during the football season. He has pictures of his favourite players on his bedroom wall. Danny is also a Pokémon fan. He swaps cards with his school friends. At home, he has a dog called Sadie and a cat called Pepper.

When Danny was six years old, he began to feel tired and sleepy a lot of the time. He also felt very thirsty and needed to drink lots of water. That meant he kept having to leave the classroom to use the toilet. Danny's dad took him to see the doctor. The doctor examined Danny and then he did lots of tests. He took a sample of Danny's blood with a needle. The blood sample showed that Danny's blood had too much sugar in it. The doctor explained that this meant that Danny had **diabetes**.

Diabetes is not catching. It means that someone may have too much or too little sugar in their blood. If they have too much sugar, they will feel sleepy and thirsty all the time. If they have too little sugar, they will feel tired, hungry and shaky.

The amount of sugar in our blood is controlled by a **chemical** called **insulin**. When we eat, insulin turns the food into sugars that give us energy. Normally, our bodies make all the insulin they need. But when someone has diabetes, their body may not be making enough insulin. People who are **diabetic** may need to have injections of insulin.

When his doctor found out he was diabetic, Danny had to go into hospital. He had to have insulin injected into his hand until he felt better. Now Danny has to check his blood sugar several times a day. He pricks his finger to do the **blood sugar test**. It takes him less than a minute.

Danny has also learned how to give himself injections of insulin. When he is older, he wants to use an insulin pump. The pump will give him all the insulin he needs when he punches in a number.

Some people inject the insulin they need.

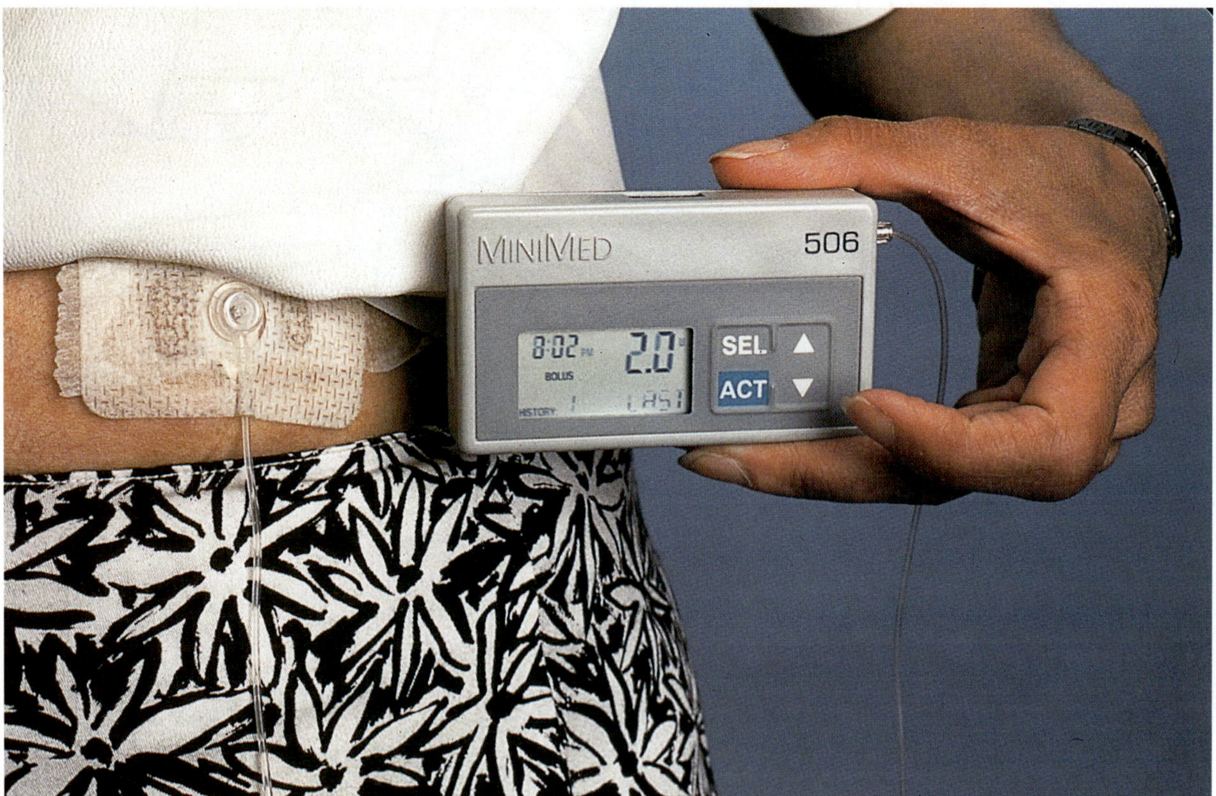

Insulin pumps are very easy to use.

Danny has to be careful to eat regular meals even if he isn't hungry. If he gets hungry, or uses up too much energy when he is playing football, his blood sugar can get low and he starts to feel tired and shaky. He drinks a glass of fruit juice and eats a **glucose** tablet to make him feel better.

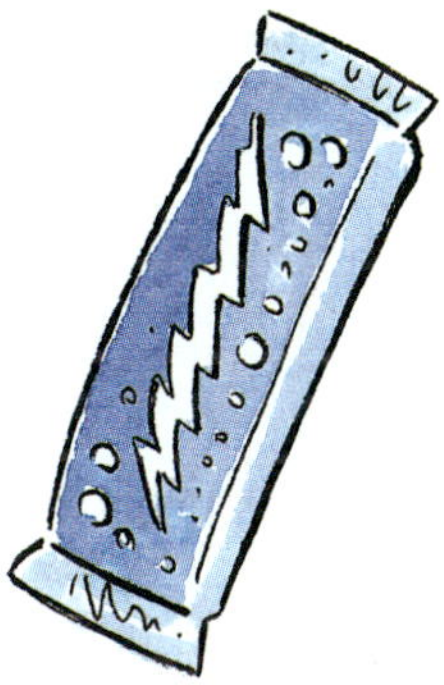

It helps to eat snacks through the day but Danny has to be careful not to eat too many sugary foods, like chocolates and sweets. They could make his blood sugar level too high, and make him feel sleepy and thirsty. Then he needs to drink water and inject more insulin. It is better not to eat too many chocolates. Danny says this is the worst thing about having diabetes!

Janine Has Leukaemia

Janine likes listening to her favourite CDs and looking after her pet rabbit Lucy. Sometimes, her friends come over and bring their CDs so they can listen together in Janine's bedroom. Janine has posters of all her favourite bands on her bedroom walls.

Janine is nine years old. When she was seven she began to feel tired all the time, and she looked very pale. She began to miss school because she didn't feel well. Her mum knew something was wrong so she took Janine to see the doctor. Janine's doctor examined her. Then he decided to do some tests on her blood. Janine had to be very brave while the doctor took samples of her blood with a needle.

The blood tests showed that Janine had **leukaemia**. Leukaemia is a disease but it is not catching. It means that Janine's blood is not healthy. It cannot help her fight off diseases and **germs** properly. Leukaemia is sometimes called "blood cancer".

Our blood contains different kinds of **cells**. Red cells carry oxygen round the blood while white cells fight germs and diseases. Blood cells are made in our bone marrow, which is the soft spongy stuff inside our bones. When someone has leukaemia, bad cells spread in their blood and crowd out the healthy cells. The blood may not have enough red cells to carry oxygen to the heart and other parts of our body which need it. There may not be enough white cells to fight off illnesses.

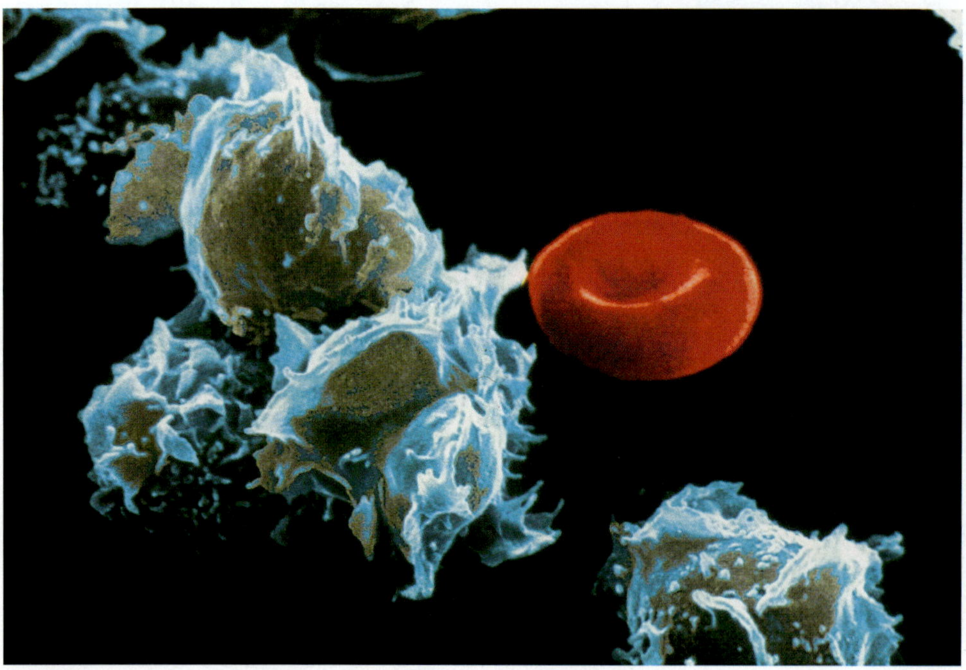

Bad white blood cells and one healthy red blood cell.

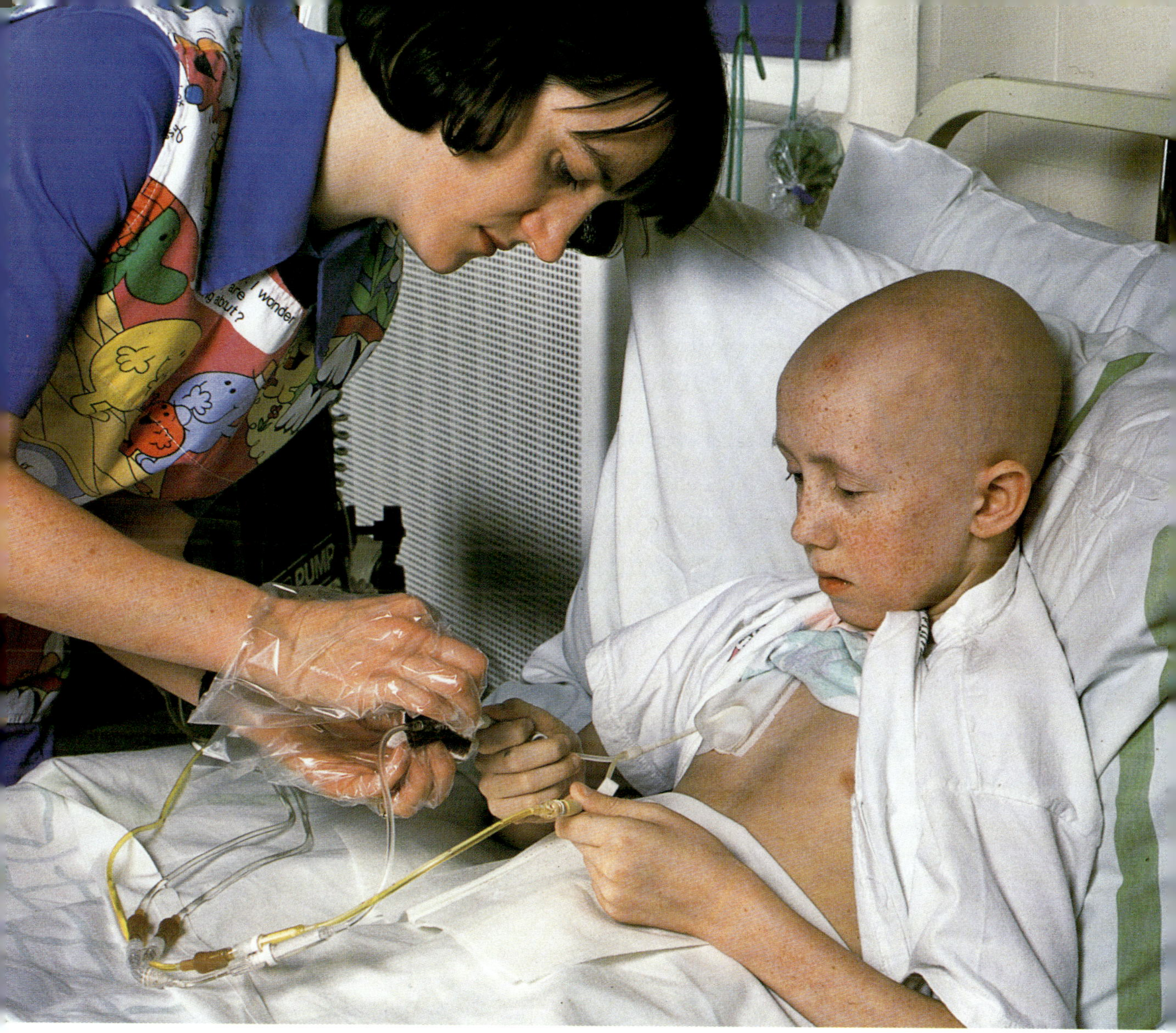

Special drugs are used to fight the bad white blood cells.

When Janine's family were told she had leukaemia they felt very worried. The doctor told them Janine needed special drugs and treatment to fight the blood cancer and make her better. Some of the drugs she has to take have made her hair fall out but Janine knows it will grow back. She also has to have **radiotherapy** treatment. This makes her feel very tired.

Janine has to miss a lot of school so she can rest and have treatment. She has to spend a lot of time in hospital. All the nurses on the ward know her and they look after her very well. They make sure that Janine has some of her favourite things around her when she is in hospital. She takes her CD player too, so she can listen to her favourite music.

The doctors have told Janine that she needs to have an operation. This is called a bone marrow transplant. This will take out all the bad cells in her blood and replace them with healthy cells.

When Janine is in hospital, her friends visit her and bring her CDs and other treats to cheer her up. After she has had her operation, they are hoping that one of her favourite pop stars will visit her. Janine is very excited about that.

Janine's grandad has told her he will take her to Disneyworld in Florida when she is feeling better. She is excited about that, too!

Glossary

backbone	the long bone that runs down your back
blood sugar test	a way of measuring how much sugar there is in the blood
braces	supports
breathing	the way you take air into your body
cells	the tiny living bits that make up your body
chemical	a substance – some chemicals are found in your body
chest physical treatment	a way of clearing sticky stuff out of the lungs
cystic fibrosis	when salt and water are not carried around the body properly
deaf	someone who cannot hear
diabetes	when someone has too much or too little sugar in their blood
diabetic	a person who has diabetes
digest	to break down food into smaller pieces
finger spelling	using your fingers and hands to spell out words
germs	tiny living things that can make you ill
glucose	a type of sugar
hearing aid	worn in the ear to make sounds louder
infection	when germs get inside your body
insulin	the chemical that turns food into sugars that give us energy
leukaemia	a disease which is sometimes called blood cancer
lip reading	making out the words someone is saying by watching their lips